Livewire Shakespeare

William Shakespeare's

Much Ado About Nothing

EDITED BY
Philip Page and Marilyn Pettit

ILLUSTRATED BY
Philip Page

Published in association with

The
Basic Skills
Agency

Hodder Murray

Orders: please contact Bookpoint Ltd, 130 Milton Park, Abingdon, Oxon OX14 4SB.
Telephone: (44) 01235 827720. Fax: (44) 01235 400454. Lines are open from
9.00 am to 6.00 pm, Monday to Saturday, with a 24-hour message answering
service. Visit our website at www.hoddereducation.co.uk

A catalogue record for this title is available from the British Library

ISBN-10 0 340 88808 3
ISBN-13 9 780340 88808 7

First published in 2005 by
Hodder Murray, a member of the Hodder Headline Group
338 Euston Road
London NW1 3BH

Impression number	10 9 8 7 6 5 4 3 2 1
Year	2010 2009 2008 2007 2006 2005

Cover illustration by Dave Smith
Typeset by DC Graphic Design Limited, Swanley, Kent
Printed in Great Britain by J W Arrowsmith Ltd, Bristol

Hodder Headline's policy is to use papers that are natural, renewable and recyclable
products and made from wood grown in sustainable forests. The logging and
manufacturing processes conform to the environmental regulations of the country
of origin.

Contents

About the play

Much Ado About Nothing is a romantic comedy.

Shakespeare's comedies all follow a formula. This means that the audience knows that however many bad things happen, everything will be resolved in the end. His comedies usually end in a wedding and a party.

In this comedy, a young woman is wrongly accused of being a whore. Worse still, it is her future husband who charges her with this at the altar, minutes before they are going to marry! To prove her innocence, she has to fake her own death. Some men don't seem to care about her; while others are more worried about their reputations.

While these potentially tragic events are taking place, another two people find love. Read on to find out how something this sinister ends in a double celebration.

As you read, list the number of times people eavesdrop, overhear, believe rumours, watch others – in other words '*note things*'. Decide whether you agree with some readers, who think that Shakespeare meant a pun (word play) on the words 'noting' and 'nothing' so that the play could be 'Much Ado About Noting'!

Is the phrase 'romantic comedy' an appropriate description of the play?

Cast of characters

Don Pedro
Prince of Aragon

Don John
Don Pedro's bastard
brother

Leonato
Governor of Messina

Hero
Leonato's daughter

Antonio
Leonato's brother

Beatrice
Leonato's niece

Ursula

Margaret

Hero's servants

Claudio
A young lord of
Florence

Benedick
A young lord of
Padua

Conrade   **Borachio**
Two of Don John's men

Friar Francis

Balthasar
A musician

Dogberry
The Constable

Verges
Dogberry's assistant

Francis Seacole
The Town Clerk

A messenger

vi

Soldiers, including Don Pedro and Claudio, arrive at Leonato's house in Messina. They stay as his guests and one of them falls in love.

I learn in this letter that Don Pedro of Aragon comes this night to Messina.

He is very near.

How many gentlemen have you lost in this action?

Few of any sort, and none of name.

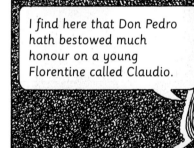

I find here that Don Pedro hath bestowed much honour on a young Florentine called Claudio.

Much deserved on his part. He hath borne himself beyond the promise of his age, doing, in the figure of a lamb, the feats of a lion.

He hath an uncle here in Messina will be very much glad of it.

I have already delivered him letters, and there appears much joy in him.

Is **Signior Mountanto** returned from the wars or no?

Signior Mountanto – 'Mr Swordfighter'

1

I know none of that name, lady.

My cousin means Signior Benedick of Padua.

O, he's returned, and as pleasant as ever he was. He hath done good service, lady, in these wars.

A good soldier too, lady.

A good soldier to a lady, but what is he to a lord?

A lord to a lord, a man to a man, stuffed with all honourable virtues.

He is no less than a stuffed man; but for the stuffing – well, we are all mortal.

You must not, sir, mistake my niece. There is a kind of merry war betwixt Signior Benedick and her: they never meet but there's a **skirmish of wit** between them.

Who is his companion now? He hath every month a new sworn brother. He wears his faith but as the fashion of his hat, it ever changes.

Skirmish of wit – battle of wits, clever word play

ere a – before he
your trouble – those who are going to inconvenience you

Act 1 Scene 1	A battle of wits takes place between Benedick and Beatrice.

Benedick: If Signior Leonato be her father, she would not have his head on her shoulders for all Messina, as like him as she is. *[Don Pedro and Leonato talk aside.]*

Beatrice: I wonder that you will still be talking, Signior Benedick: nobody **marks you**.

is listening to you

Benedick: What! Are you yet living?
It is certain I am loved of all ladies, only you excepted.

Beatrice: I had rather hear my dog bark at a crow than a man swears he loves me.

Benedick: God keep your ladyship still in that mind, so some gentleman or other shall scape a scratched face.

Beatrice: Scratching could not make it worse, and 'twere such a face as yours were.

Benedick: Well, you are a rare **parrot-teacher**.

someone who repeats silly comments

Beatrice: A bird of my tongue is better than a beast of yours.

Benedick: I would my horse had the speed of your tongue. But **keep your way**, I have done.

keep quiet now

Beatrice: You always **end with a jade's trick**, I know you of old.

manage to wriggle your way out

Think about it

When two people insult each other in this way, do they *really* dislike each other?

4

being reconciled to — having made peace with

6

I shall see thee, ere I die, look pale with love.

With anger, with sickness, or with hunger, my lord, not with love.

'In time the savage bull doth bear the yoke.'

In the meantime, Signior Benedick, repair to Leonato's and tell him I will not fail him at supper.

Hath Leonato any son, my lord?

No child but Hero, she's his only heir.

If thou dost love fair Hero, I will **break** with her, and with her father, and thou shalt have her.

We shall have **revelling** tonight: I will assume some disguise, and tell fair Hero I am Claudio. I'll unclasp my heart, then after to her father will I break, and she shall be thine.

break – talk
revelling – partying

Leonato is told that the Prince, Don Pedro, loves his daughter.

How now, brother?

I can tell you strange news.

The Prince and Count Claudio were overheard by a man of mine: the Prince discovered to Claudio that he loved your daughter, and meant to acknowledge it this night in a dance.

Hath the fellow any wit that told you this?

A good sharp fellow.

I will acquaint my daughter withal. Go and tell her of it.

Hath the fellow any wit – Is the man reliable?

Don John proves he still hates his brother. He and his men plan to cause trouble for both Don Pedro and Claudio.

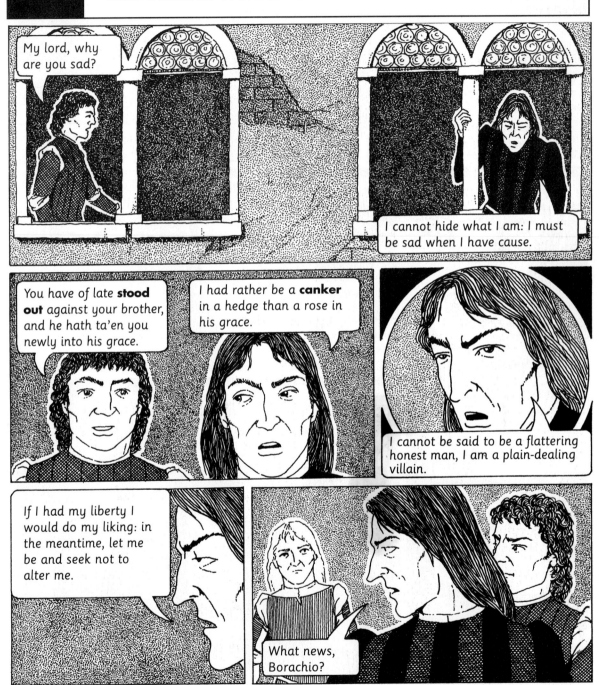

stood out – fought
canker – wild rose

I can give you intelligence of an intended marriage.

Will it serve for any model to build mischief on?

It is your brother's right hand.

Who, the most exquisite Claudio?

Which way looks he?

On Hero, the daughter and heir of Leonato.

How came you to this?

I heard it that the Prince should woo Hero for himself, and having obtained her, give her to Count Claudio.

This may prove food to my displeasure. If I can cross him any way, I bless myself every way. You will assist me?

To the death, my lord.

Act 2 Scene 1	Hero is told what to say and how to behave. Beatrice makes clear her views on marriage, while Benedick makes clear his views on Beatrice.

Was Count John here at supper?

I saw him not.

How tartly that gentleman looks! I never can see him but I am heart-burned an hour after.

He is of a very melancholy disposition.

He were an excellent man that were made in the mid-way between him and Benedick: the one says nothing, and the other evermore tattling.

Thou wilt never get a husband, if thou be so **shrewd of thy tongue**.

God send me no husband. Lord, I could not endure a husband!

shrewd of thy tongue – sarcastic

11

Well, niece, I trust you will be ruled by your father.

It is my cousin's duty to make curtsy and say, 'Father, as it please you'.

But for all that, cousin, let him be a handsome fellow, or else make another curtsy and say, 'Father, as it please me'.

I hope to see you one day fitted with a husband.

Not till God make men of some other metal than earth.

Daughter, remember what I told you: if the Prince **do solicit you in that kind**, you know your answer.

Hero: wooing, wedding, and repenting is as a **Scotch jig, a measure, and a cinque-pace**: the first is hot and hasty; the wedding modest as a measure; and then comes repentance and, with his bad legs, falls into the cinque-pace faster and faster, till he sink into his grave.

The revellers are entering; make room.

do solicit ... kind – proposes to you
Scotch jig ... cinque-pace – dances

Lady, will you **walk a bout** with your friend?

I am yours for the walk.

I would you did like me.

So would not I for your own sake, for I have many ill qualities.

Which is one?

I say my prayers aloud.

I love you the better.

walk a bout – dance

13

I know you, you are Signior Antonio.

I am not. I counterfeit him.

You could never do him so ill-well. You are he and there's an end.

Will you not tell me who told you that I was disdainful?

Signior Benedick said so.

What's he?

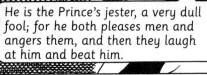

He is the Prince's jester, a very dull fool; for he both pleases men and angers them, and then they laugh at him and beat him.

I'll tell him what you say.

Do.

We must follow the leaders.

<table>
<tr><td>

**Act 2
Scene 1**

</td><td>

Meanwhile, Claudio is tricked into believing that Don Pedro has declared his love for Hero, but he soon learns the truth.

</td></tr>
</table>

Don John: Sure my brother is amorous on Hero, and hath withdrawn her father to break with him about it. The ladies follow her, and but one **visor** remains.

masked person

Borachio: And that is Claudio: I know him by his **bearing**.

the way he moves

Don John: Are you not Signior Benedick?

Claudio: I am he.

Don John: Signior, you are very near my brother in his love. He is **enamoured on** Hero; I pray you, dissuade him from her, she is no equal to his birth.

in love with

Claudio: How know you he loves her?

Don John: I heard him swear his affection.

Borachio: So did I too, and he swore he would marry her tonight.

[Don John and Borachio leave]

Claudio: Thus answer I in name of Benedick, but hear these ill news with the ears of Claudio. 'Tis certain so; the Prince woos for himself. Friendship is constant in all other things save in the office and affairs of love. Farewell, therefore, Hero!

[Enter Benedick]

Benedick: Count Claudio?

Claudio: Yea, the same.

Benedick: Come, will you go with me **to the next willow**? What fashion will you wear the garland? You must wear it one way, for the Prince hath got your Hero.

The willow tree was a symbol of lost love.

15

Claudio: I wish him joy of her.

Benedick: Did you think the Prince would have **served you thus?**

treated you like that

Claudio: I pray you, leave me.

Benedick: You strike like the blind man! 'Twas the boy that stole your meat, and you'll beat the post.

Don't be angry at me because I tell you what Don Pedro's done.

Claudio: I'll leave you.   [*Claudio leaves*]

Benedick: Poor hurt fowl, now will he creep into **sedges**. But that my Lady Beatrice should know me, and not know me! The Prince's fool! Ha, it may be I go under that title because I am merry. It is the base, though bitter, disposition of Beatrice that puts the world into her person, and so gives me out. Well, I'll be revenged as I may.

waterside reeds

Think about it

What does Claudio's reaction to the news tell you about his character?

poniards – daggers
terminations – descriptions of me

I will go on the slightest errand now rather than hold three words' conference with this **harpy**. You have no employment for me?

None.

Lady, you have lost the heart of Signior Benedick.

Indeed, my lord, he lent it me awhile, and I gave him use for it.

Once before he won it of me with false dice, therefore your Grace may well say I have lost it.

I have brought Count Claudio, whom you sent me to seek.

Count? Wherefore are you sad?

Claudio, I have wooed in thy name, and fair Hero is won. I have broke with her father, and his good will obtained.

Name the day of marriage, and God give thee joy!

harpy – monster

Count, take of me my daughter, and with her my fortunes; his Grace hath made the match.

Lady, as you are mine, I am yours.

Good Lord, for **alliance**! Thus goes everyone but I. I may sit in a corner and cry 'Heigh-ho for a husband!'

Lady Beatrice, I will get you one. Will you have me, lady?

No, my lord: your Grace is too costly to wear every day.

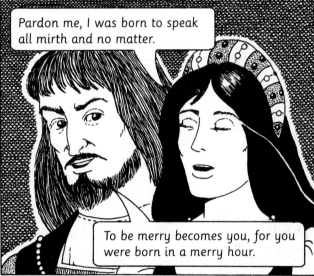

Pardon me, I was born to speak all mirth and no matter.

To be merry becomes you, for you were born in a merry hour.

No, my lord, my mother cried, but then there was a star danced, and under that was I born.

Niece, will you look to those things I told you of?

alliance – marriage

19

A plan is hatched to bring Benedick and Beatrice together.

Beatrice: By your Grace's pardon.

[*Beatrice leaves*]

Don Pedro: A pleasant-spirited lady.

Leonato: There's little of the **melancholy** element in her;   sad
she is never sad but when she sleeps and not ever then for
I have heard my daughter say she hath often waked
herself with laughing.

Don Pedro: She cannot endure to hear tell of a husband.

Leonato: O, by no means, she mocks all her wooers out
of suit.

Don Pedro: She were an excellent wife for Benedick.

Leonato: My lord, if they were but a week married, they
would talk themselves mad.

Don Pedro: Claudio, when mean you to go to church?

Claudio: Tomorrow, my lord: time goes on crutches till
love have all his rites.

Leonato: Not till Monday, my dear son, which is just
seven-night.

Don Pedro: You shake the head at so long a breathing,
but I warrant thee, Claudio, the time shall not go dully
by us. I will, in the interim, undertake one of Hercules'
labours, which is, to bring Signior Benedick and the Lady
Beatrice into a mountain of affection th'one with th'other.
I would fain have it a match and I doubt not but to
fashion it, if you three will but minister such assistance as
I shall give you direction.

Leonato: My lord, I am for you.

Claudio: And I, my lord.

Don Pedro: And you too, gentle Hero?

Hero: I will do any modest office, my lord, to help my cousin to a good husband.

Don Pedro: And Benedick is not the unhopefullest husband that I know. Thus far can I praise him: he is **of a noble strain**, **of approved valour**, and confirmed honesty. I will teach you how to humour your cousin that she shall fall in love with Benedick; and I [*to Leonato and Claudio*] with your two helps, will so practise on Benedick that, in despite of his quick wit and queasy stomach, he shall fall in love with Beatrice. Go in with me, and I will tell you my **drift**.

from a good family

brave

plan

Think about it

Is there any previous evidence to suggest that this plan might work?

**Act 2
Scene 2** | Borachio shares his evil scheme with
Don John, and Hero's fate is sealed.

[Enter Don John and Borachio]

Don John: It is so, the Count Claudio shall marry the daughter of Leonato.

Borachio: Yea, my lord, but I can **cross it**.

prevent it

Don John: How canst thou cross this marriage?

Borachio: Not honestly, my lord, but so **covertly** that no dishonesty shall appear in me.

secretly

Don John: Show me briefly how.

Borachio: I think I told your lordship how much I am in favour of Margaret, the waiting-gentlewoman to Hero.

Don John: I remember.

Borachio: I can, at any instant of the night, **appoint** her to look out at her lady's chamber-window.

persuade

Don John: What life is in that, to be the death of this marriage?

Borachio: The poison of that lies in you to **temper**. Go you to the Prince your brother; spare not to tell him that he hath wronged his honour in marrying the renowned Claudio – whose estimation do you mightily hold up – to a **contaminated stale**, such a one as Hero.

make

whore

Don John: What proof shall I make of that?

Borachio: Proof enough to misuse the Prince, to vex Claudio, to undo Hero, and kill Leonato. Look you for any other issue?

Don John: Only to despite them I will endeavour anything.

Borachio: Go then, find me a **meet hour** to draw Don   suitable time
Pedro and the Count Claudio alone: tell them that you
know that Hero loves me; intend a kind of zeal both to
the Prince and Claudio – as in love of your brother's
honour, who hath made this match, and his friend's
reputation, who is thus like to be **cozened** with the   cheated
semblance of a maid – that you have discovered thus.   supposed virgin
They will scarcely believe this without trial: offer them
instances, which shall bear no less likelihood than to see
me at her chamber-window, hear me call Margaret Hero,
hear Margaret term me Claudio; and bring them to see
this very night before the intended wedding – for in the
meantime I will so fashion the matter that Hero shall be
absent – and there shall appear such seeming truth of
Hero's disloyalty that jealousy shall be called assurance
and all the preparation overthrown.

Don John: I will put it in practice. Be cunning in the
working this, and thy fee is a thousand ducats.

Borachio: Be constant in the accusation, and my cunning
shall not shame me.

Don John: I will **presently** go learn their day of   immediately
marriage.

[*They both leave*]

Think about it

Is the money the only reason for Borachio's
plan?

Benedick listens in on a conversation that is about to change his attitude to marriage.

I wonder that one man, seeing how much another man is a fool when he dedicates his behaviours to love, will become the argument of his own scorn by falling in love: and such a man is Claudio.

Till all graces be in one woman, one woman shall not come in my grace.

Ha! the Prince and Monsieur Love! I will hide me.

See you where Benedick hath hid himself?

O, very well, my lord.

Leonato. What was it you told me today, that Beatrice was in love with Benedick?

I did never think that lady would have loved any man.

24

No, nor I, but most wonderful that she should so dote on Signior Benedick.

Is't possible?

She loves him with an enraged affection.

I should think this a **gull**, but that the **white-bearded fellow** speaks it. Knavery cannot sure hide himself in such reverence.

He hath **ta'en th'infection**; hold it up.

Hath she made her affection known to Benedick?

No, and swears she never will.

gull – con trick
white-bearded fellow – old man
ta'en th'infection – fallen for it

So your daughter says: 'Shall I,' says she, 'that have so oft encountered him with scorn, write to him that I love him?'

She'll be up twenty times a night till she have writ a sheet of paper: my daughter tells us all.

She tore the letter, railed at herself, that she should write to one that she knew would flout her.

Then upon her knees she falls, weeps, sobs, beats her heart, tears her hair, prays, curses: 'O sweet Benedick!'

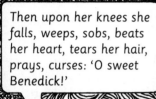

She doth indeed, my daughter says so.

It were good that Benedick knew of it by some other, if she will not discover it.

He would make but a sport of it and torment the poor lady worse.

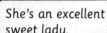

She's an excellent sweet lady.

And she is wise.

In everything but in loving Benedick.

Hero thinks she will die; for she says she will die if he love her not, and she will die ere she make her love known, and she will die if he woo her.

The man, as you know all, hath a contemptible spirit.

I am sorry for your niece. Shall we go seek Benedick, and tell him of her love?

Never tell him my lord, let her wear it out with good **counsel**.

Let it cool the while. I wish he would examine himself, to see how much he is unworthy so good a lady.

My lord. Dinner is ready.

Let there be the same net spread for her. The sport will be when they hold one an opinion of another's **dotage**.

Let us send her to call him in to dinner.

This can be no trick: they have the truth of this from Hero.

I did never think to marry. No, the world must be peopled.

counsel – advice
dotage – love-sickness

Here comes Beatrice.

She's a fair lady! I do spy some marks of love in her.

Against my will I am sent to bid you come in to dinner.

Fair Beatrice, I thank you for your pains.

I took no more pains for those thanks than you take pains to thank me; if it had been painful, I would not have come.

You take pleasure then in the message?

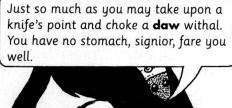

Just so much as you may take upon a knife's point and choke a **daw** withal. You have no stomach, signior, fare you well.

Ha! 'Against my will I am sent to bid you come in to dinner' – there's a double meaning in that.

'I took no more pains for those thanks than you took pains to thank me' – that's as much as to say, 'Any pains that I take for you is as easy as thanks'.

daw – jackdaw

**Act 3
Scene 1**

Beatrice overhears a conversation that will change her view of Benedick!

Margaret, find my cousin Beatrice, tell her I and Ursley walk in the orchard, and our whole discourse is all of her.

I'll make her come.

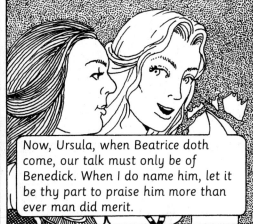

Now, Ursula, when Beatrice doth come, our talk must only be of Benedick. When I do name him, let it be thy part to praise him more than ever man did merit.

My talk to thee must be how Benedick is sick in love with Beatrice.

Now go we near her, that her ear lose nothing.

Are you sure that Benedick loves Beatrice?

So says the Prince and my **new-trothed lord**. But I persuaded them never to let Beatrice know of it.

Why?

She cannot love, she is so self-endeared.

new-trothed lord – fiancé

29

Certainly it were not good she knew his love, lest she'll make sport at it.

Who dare tell her so? If I should speak, she would mock me.

Yet tell her of it; hear what she will say.

No; I will go to Benedick and counsel him to fight against his passion; I'll devise some honest slanders to stain my cousin.

Do not do your cousin such a wrong! She cannot be so much without true judgement to refuse so rare a gentleman as Signior Benedick.

Indeed he hath an excellent good name.

When are you married, madam?

Tomorrow! Come, go in.

We have caught her, madam.

What fire is in mine ears? Can this be true? Stand I condemn'd for pride and scorn so much?

Benedick, love on, I will **requite thee**. If thou dost love, my kindness shall incite thee to bind our loves up in a holy band.

requite thee – return your love

30

Act 3 Scene 2

Don Pedro, Claudio and Leonato notice Benedick's change of mood.

I do but stay till your marriage be consummate, and then go I toward Aragon with Benedick for company, for he is all mirth.

I am not as I have been.

Methinks you are sadder.

I hope he be in love.

There's no true drop of blood in him to be truly touched with love. If he be sad, he wants money.

I have toothache.

What? Sigh for the toothache?

Well, every one can master a grief but he that has it.

He is in love. Nay, but I know who loves him.

One that knows him not.

Yet is this no charm for the toothache. Old signior, walk with me; I have wise words to speak to you.

To break with him about Beatrice.

Hero and Margaret have by this played their parts with Beatrice, and then the two bears will not bite one another when they meet.

<table>
<tr><td>

**Act 3
Scene 2**
</td><td>

Don John's lies convince Claudio and
Don Pedro to meet him at midnight
when he will prove Hero is a whore.
</td></tr>
</table>

[*Enter Don John*]

Don John: My lord and brother, God save you!

Don Pedro: Good **den**, brother.   morning

Don John: **If your leisure served**, I would speak with you.   If you have time

Don Pedro: In private?

Don John: If it please you; yet Count Claudio may hear,
for what I speak of concerns him.

Don Pedro: What's the matter?

Don John: [*To Claudio*] Means your lordship to be
married tomorrow?

Don Pedro: You know he does.

Don John: I know not that, when he knows what I know.

Claudio: If there be any **impediment**, I pray you **discover** it.   obstacle   tell

Don John: You may think I love you not: let that appear
hereafter, and aim better at me by that I now will
manifest. For my brother, I think he holds you well, and   show
in dearness of heart hath **holp** to effect your ensuing   helped
marriage – surely suit ill spent and labour ill bestowed.

Don Pedro: Why, what's the matter?

Don John: I came hither to tell you; and, circumstances
shortened – for she has been too long a-talking of – the
lady is disloyal.

Claudio: Who, Hero?

Don John: Even she – Leonato's Hero, your Hero, every
man's Hero.

Claudio: Disloyal?

Don John: The word is too good to paint out her wickedness. I could say she were worse; think you of a worse title and I will fit her to it. Wonder not **till further warrant**: go but with me tonight, you shall see her chamber-window entered, even the night before her wedding-day. If you love her then, tomorrow wed her; but it would better fit your honour to change your mind.

until you see the proof

Claudio: May this be so?

Don Pedro: I will not think it.

Don John: If you dare not trust that you see, confess not that you know. If you will follow me, I will show you enough; and when you have seen more, and heard more, proceed accordingly.

> ## Think about it
>
> Why do Don Pedro and Claudio accept Don John's word so quickly?

Claudio: If I see anything tonight why I should not marry her tomorrow, in the congregation, where I should wed, there will I shame her.

Don Pedro: And as I wooed for thee to obtain her, I will join with thee to disgrace her.

Don John: I will disparage her no farther till you are my witnesses. **Bear it coldly** but till midnight, and let the issue show itself.

Keep calm

Don Pedro: O day untowardly turned!

Claudio: O mischief strangely thwarting!

Don John: O plague right well prevented! So will you say when you have seen **the sequel**.   [*They all leave*]

what happens next

Act 3 Scene 3

Dogberry, the Constable, gives the Watch their orders for the night.

Are you good men and true?

Yea. Give them their charge, Dogberry.

This is your charge: you shall comprehend all **vagrom** men.

You shall also make no noise in the streets.

You are to call at all the ale-houses, and bid those that are drunk get them to bed.

If you hear a child cry, you must call to the nurse and bid her still it.

We hear our charge: let us go sit here upon the church-bench till two, and then all to bed.

One word more. Watch about Signior Leonato's door, for the wedding being there tomorrow, there is a great **coil** tonight.

vagrom – vagrant/beggar
coil – commotion

34

Conrade!

Peace! Stir not.

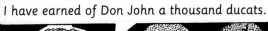

I have earned of Don John a thousand ducats.

I have tonight wooed Margaret, the Lady Hero's gentlewoman, by the name of Hero.

She leans out at her mistress's chamber-window, bids me a thousand times good night – I should tell thee how the Prince, Claudio, and my master, planted and placed and possessed by my master Don John, saw afar this encounter.

And thought they Margaret was Hero?

Two of them did, the Prince and Claudio, but the devil my master knew she was Margaret.

Away went Claudio enraged; swore he would meet her next morning at the temple, and there, before the whole congregation, shame her and send her home again without a husband.

We charge you in the Prince's name, stand!

Call up the Master Constable; we have here recovered the most dangerous piece of lechery.

Never speak, go with us.

We'll obey you.

Hero prepares for her wedding. Beatrice realises she is in love!

Good morrow, **coz**. Do you speak in the sick tune?

I am out of all other tune.

I am sick.

Get you some of this distilled carduus benedictus, it is the only thing for a qualm.

You have some moral in this benedictus.

No, I meant plain holy-thistle. You may think perchance that I think you are in love, nay, I am not such a fool to think that you are in love.

Yet Benedick was such another and he swore he would never marry, and yet now in despite of his heart he eats his meal without grudging.

Methinks you look with your eyes as other women do.

Madam! The Prince, the Count, Signior Benedick, Don John, and all the gallants of the town are come to fetch you to church.

Help to dress me.

coz – cousin

36

Leonato is too busy to learn the truth from the Watch.

What would you with me, honest neighbour?

I would have some confidence with you.

Brief, I pray you, for you see it is a busy time with me.

Our watch, sir, have comprehended two persons, and we would have them this morning examined before your worship.

Take their examination yourself, and bring it me; I am now in great haste.

My lord, they stay for you to give your daughter to her husband.

I'll wait upon them; I am ready.

Get Francis Seacole, bid him bring his pen and inkhorn to the gaol: we are now to examination these men.

Act 4
Scene 1

The wedding is called off when Hero's reputation is questioned.

You come, my lord, to marry this lady?

No.

To be married to her, friar: you come to marry her.

Lady, you come to be married to this Count?

I do.

If either of you know of any **inward impediment** why you should not be **conjoined**, I charge you on your souls to utter it.

Know you any, Hero?

None, my lord.

Know you any, Count?

I dare make his answer, None.

Will you with free and unconstrained soul, give me this maid, your daughter?

As freely as God did give her to me.

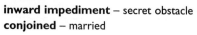

inward impediment – secret obstacle
conjoined – married

38

Leonato, take her back again.

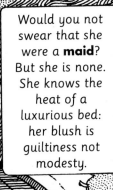

Would you not swear that she were a **maid**? But she is none. She knows the heat of a luxurious bed: her blush is guiltiness not modesty.

What do you mean, my lord?

Not to be married.

If you have **vanquish'd the resistance of her youth** –

No, I never tempted her, but, as a brother to his sister, show'd sincerity and love.

Seem'd I otherwise to you?

You are more **intemperate** than Venus.

Is my lord well?

Sweet Prince, why speak you not?

What should I speak? I stand dishonour'd, to link my dear friend to a **common stale**.

Are these things spoken, or do I but dream?

Sir, these things are true.

This looks not like a **nuptial**!

maid – virgin
vanquish'd … youth – seduced her
intemperate – passionate

common stale – whore
nuptial – wedding

Hero: 'True'? O God!

Claudio: Let me but move one question to your daughter, and by that fatherly and kindly power that you have in her, bid her answer truly.

Leonato: I charge thee do so, as thou art my child.

Claudio: What man was he talk'd with you yesternight, out at your window betwixt twelve and one? Now, if you are a maid, answer to this.

Hero: I talk'd with no man at that hour, my lord.

Don Pedro: Why, then you are no maiden. Leonato, I am sorry you must hear: upon mine honour, myself, my brother, and this grieved Count did see her, hear her, at that hour last night, talk with a ruffian at her chamber-window, who hath indeed confess'd the vile encounters they have had a thousand times in secret.

Don John: They are not to be nam'd, my lord. Not to be spoke of! There is not chastity enough in language without offence to utter them. Thus, pretty lady, I am sorry for thy much misgovernment.

Claudio: What a Hero hadst thou been, if half thy outward graces had been plac'd about thy thoughts and counsels of thy heart! Farewell.

Leonato: Hath no man's dagger here a point for me?

[Hero faints]

Think about it

What do you think of Hero's father's response?

How doth the lady?

Dead, I think. Help, uncle!

Death is the fairest cover for her shame.

How now, cousin Hero?

Have comfort, lady.

Doth not every earthly thing cry shame upon her? Why ever wast thou lovely in my eyes? Why had I not with a charitable hand took up a beggar's **issue** at my gates, I might have said, 'No part of it is mine'.

She is fall'n into a pit of ink, the wide sea hath drops too few to wash her clean again.

Sir, be patient.

My cousin is belied!

Lady, were you her bedfellow last night?

No, truly not.

Confirm'd, confirm'd! Would the two princes lie, and Claudio lie, who lov'd her so?

Let her die!

issue – child

41

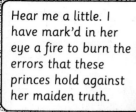 Hear me a little. I have mark'd in her eye a fire to burn the errors that these princes hold against her maiden truth.

Call me a fool; trust not my age, my reverence, calling, if this sweet lady lie not guiltless here under some biting error.

 Friar, it cannot be. She not denies it.

 Lady, what man is he you are accus'd of?

I know none.

 There is some strange **misprision** in the princes.

If their wisdoms be misled in this, the practice of it lives in John the bastard.

 If they speak but truth of her, these hands shall tear her: if they wrong her honour, the proudest of them shall well hear of it.

 Let my counsel sway you in this case. Your daughter here the princes left for dead, let her awhile be secretly kept in, and publish it that she is dead indeed, and do all rites that appertain unto a burial.

What will this do?

This shall change slander to remorse. She dying shall be pitied and excus'd. Claudio shall hear she died upon his words, then shall he mourn and wish he had not so accused her. If it sort not well, you may conceal her in **some reclusive and religious life**, out of all eyes, tongues, minds, and injuries.

 Signior Leonato, let the friar advise you; and though you know my love is unto the Prince and Claudio, I will deal in this secretly.

 Come, lady, die to live; this wedding-day perhaps is but prolong'd; have patience and endure.

misprision – mistake/misunderstanding
some ... life – a convent

Benedick: Lady Beatrice, have you wept all this while?

Beatrice: Yea, and I will weep a while longer.

Benedick: Surely, I do believe your fair cousin is wronged.

Beatrice: How much might the man deserve of me that would right her!

Benedick: Is there any way to show such friendship?

Beatrice: A very **even** way, but no such friend.   easy

Benedick: May a man do it?

Beatrice: It is a man's **office**, but not yours.   job

Benedick: I do love nothing in the world so well as you – is not that strange?

Beatrice: As strange as the thing I know not. It were as possible for me to say I loved nothing so well as you, but believe me or not; and yet I lie not; I confess nothing, nor I deny nothing. I am sorry for my cousin.

Benedick: By my sword, Beatrice, thou lovest me.

Beatrice: Do not swear it and **eat it**.   later deny it

Benedick: I will swear by it that you love me, and I will make him eat it that says I love not you.

Beatrice: You have **stayed me** in a happy hour, I was   met me
about to protest I loved you.

Benedick: And do it with all thy heart.

Beatrice: I love you with so much of my heart that none is left to protest.

Benedick: Come, bid me do anything for thee.

Beatrice: Kill Claudio!

Benedick: Not for the wide world!

Beatrice: You kill me to deny it. Farewell.

Benedick: Tarry, sweet Beatrice.   Wait

Beatrice: I am gone; there is no love in you.

Benedick: We'll be friends first.

Beatrice: You dare easier be friends with me than fight with mine enemy.

Benedick: Is Claudio thine enemy?

Beatrice: A villain that hath slandered, scorned, dishonoured my kinswoman? O that I were a man! I would eat his heart in the market-place.

Benedick: Hear me, Beatrice—-

Beatrice: Talk with a man out at a window! **A proper saying!** Sweet Hero! She is wronged, she is slandered, she is undone! O that I were a man or that I had any friend would be a man for my sake! I cannot be a man with wishing, therefore I will die a woman with grieving.   A likely story!

Benedick: Think you in your soul the Count Claudio hath wronged Hero?

Beatrice: Yea, as sure as I have a thought, or a soul.

Benedick: Enough! I will challenge him. Go comfort your cousin; I must say she is dead: and so farewell.

Think about it

Is Beatrice's request fair? Is she behaving irrationally or does this prove her loyalty to Hero?

**Act 4
Scene 2**

Borachio and Conrade appear before the Town Clerk and the plot to disgrace Hero is revealed.

Which are the offenders that are to be examined? Let them come before Master Constable.

What is your name?

Borachio.

Conrade.

Call the watch that are their accusers.

This man said, sir, that Don John was a villain.

Write down 'Prince John a villain'.

What heard you him say else?

That he had received a thousand ducats of Don John for accusing the Lady Hero wrongfully.

Prince John is this morning secretly stolen away: Hero was in this manner accused, and upon the grief of this suddenly died. Let these men be bound and brought to Leonato's.

You are an ass!

Bring him away! O that I had been writ down an ass!

45

Act 5 Scene 1

Leonato and Benedick realise the seriousness of the situation. Surprisingly, Don Pedro and Claudio don't seem to care!

If you go on thus, you will kill yourself.

Give me no counsel: my griefs cry louder than advertisement. My soul doth tell me Hero is belied; and that shall Claudio know, the Prince, and all of them that dishonour her.

Here comes the Prince and Claudio.

Hear you, my lords—

We have some haste, Leonato.

Are you so hasty now?

Nay, do not quarrel with us, good old man.

Claudio, thou hast so wrong'd mine innocent child and me, that I do challenge thee to **trial of a man**. She lies buried in a tomb fram'd by thy villainy!

You say not right, old man.

Away! I will not have to do with you.

Thou hast kill'd my child; if thou kill'st me, boy, thou shalt kill a man.

He shall kill two of us, and men indeed.

Gentlemen, my heart is sorry for your daughter's death; but on my honour she was charg'd with nothing but what was true, and very full of proof.

trial of a man – a duel

Here comes the man we went to seek.

Welcome; you are almost come to **part a fray**.

We had like to have had our two noses snapped off with two old men without teeth.

We are melancholy and would have it beaten away. Will thou use thy wit?

It is in my scabbard; shall I draw it?

Art thou sick, or angry?

I pray you choose another subject.

Shall I speak a word in your ear? You have killed a sweet lady, and her death shall fall heavy on you. Let me hear from you.

Beatrice praised thy wit the other day. She concluded thou wast the properest man in Italy.

I will leave you now to your gossip-like humour. I must discontinue your company. Your brother the bastard is fled. You have among you killed a sweet and innocent lady. For my Lord Lackbeard there, he and I shall meet; and till then, peace be with him.

He is in earnest. And hath challenged thee.

part a fray – stop a fight

47

Borachio confesses and Claudio agrees
to Leonato's suggestion.

Don Pedro: How now? Two of my brother's men bound? Officers, what offence have these men done?

Dogberry: Marry, sir, they have committed false report, moreover they have spoken untruths, secondarily they are slanders, sixth and lastly they have belied a lady, thirdly they have verified unjust things, and to conclude, they are lying knaves.

Don Pedro: Who have you offended? This learned constable is too cunning to be understood. What's your offence?

Borachio: Sweet Prince, hear me and let this Count kill me. What your wisdoms could not discover, these shallow fools have brought to light, how Don John incensed me to slander the Lady Hero, how you were brought into the orchard and saw me court Margaret in Hero's garments, how you disgraced her when you should marry her. The lady is dead upon mine and my master's false accusation; I desire nothing but the reward of a villain.

Don Pedro: Runs not this speech like iron through your blood?

Claudio: I have drunk poison whiles he utter'd it.

Don Pedro: But did my brother set thee on to this?

Borachio: Yea, and paid me richly for the practice of it.

Don Pedro: He is compos'd and fram'd of treachery, and fled he is upon this villainy.

Claudio: Sweet Hero! Now thy image doth appear in the rare semblance that I lov'd it first.

Dogberry: Come, bring away the plaintiffs. By this time our sexton hath reformed Signior Leonato of the matter: and masters, do not forget to specify, when time and place shall serve, that I am an ass.

> [*Enter Leonato and Antonio with the Sexton*]

Leonato: Which is the villain?

Borachio: Look on me.

Leonato: Art thou the slave that with thy breath hast kill'd mine innocent child?

Borachio: Yea, even I alone.

Leonato: No, not so. Here stand a pair of honourable men – a third is fled – that had a hand in it. I thank you, Princes, for my daughter's death; record it with your high and worthy deeds; 'Twas bravely done, if you bethink you of it.

Claudio: I know not how to pray your patience, yet I must speak. Impose me to what penance your invention can lay upon my sin; yet sinn'd I not but in mistaking.

Don Pedro: By my soul, nor I: and yet, to satisfy this good old man, I would bend under any heavy weight that he'll enjoin me to.

Leonato: I cannot bid you bid my daughter live – that were impossible – but I pray you **possess the people** in Messina here how innocent she died and hang her an epitaph upon her tomb. And since you could not be my son-in-law, be yet my nephew. My brother hath a daughter, almost the copy of my child that's dead. Give her the right you should have giv'n her cousin, and so dies my revenge.

tell the people

Claudio: Your overkindness doth wring tears from me! I do embrace your offer.

Leonato: Tomorrow then I will expect your coming; tonight I shall take my leave. This naughty man shall face to face be brought to Margaret, who I believe was pack'd in all this wrong, hir'd to it by your brother.

Borachio: No, by my soul she was not, nor knew not what she did when she spoke to me.

Dogberry: The offender did call me ass; I beseech you let it be remembered in his punishment.

Leonato: I thank thee for thy care and honest pains. I discharge thee of thy prisoner.

Dogberry: I leave an arrant knave with your worship. God keep your worship.

[*Dogberry and Verges leave*]

Leonato: Until tomorrow morning, lords, farewell.

Don Pedro: We will not fail.

Claudio: Tonight I'll mourn with Hero.

Think about it

Can you explain the humour that Dogberry brings to this scene?

Benedick and Beatrice finally accept they love each other and hear some good news.

Margaret, I pray thee call Beatrice.

Sweet Beatrice, wouldst thou come when I called thee?

Yea, and depart when you bid me.

Stay but till then!

Let me go knowing what hath passed between you and Claudio.

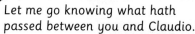

Only foul words – and thereupon I will kiss thee.

Foul words is but foul wind, and foul wind is but foul breath, and foul breath is **noisome**; therefore I will depart unkissed.

Claudio undergoes my challenge, and either I must shortly hear from him, or I will **subscribe** him a coward.

Now tell me, for which of my bad parts didst thou first fall in love with me?

For them all together. But for which of my good parts did you first suffer love?

I do suffer love indeed, for I love thee against my will.

noisome – disgusting
subscribe – call

51

In spite of your heart, I think. Alas, poor heart! If you spite it for my sake, I will spite it for yours, for I will never love that which my friend hates.

Thou and I are too wise to woo peaceably.

Now tell me, how doth your cousin?

Very ill.

And how do you?

Very ill too.

Serve God, love me, and mend. There will I leave you too, for here comes one in haste.

Madam, you must come to your uncle. It is proved my Lady Hero hath been falsely accused, the Prince and Claudio mightily abused, and Don John is the author of all, who is fled and gone. Will you come?

Will you go hear this news, signior?

I will live in thy heart, die in thy lap, and be buried in thy eyes; and moreover, I will go with thee to thy uncle's.

| Act 5 Scene 3 | Claudio hangs an epitaph on the tomb where he thinks Hero's body lies. |

monument – family tomb
guerdon – payment
weeds – clothes

**Act 5
Scene 4**

Leonato puts the final touches to his plan and Benedick asks a favour.

Did I not tell you she was innocent?

So are the Prince and Claudio. But Margaret was in some fault for this.

I am glad that all things sort so well.

And so am I, being else by faith enforc'd to call young Claudio to a reckoning for it.

Well, daughter, and you gentlewomen all, withdraw into a chamber by yourselves, and when I send for you, come hither mask'd.

The Prince and Claudio promis'd by this hour to visit me. You know your office, brother: you must be father to your brother's daughter, and give her to young Claudio.

Friar, I must **entreat your pains**, I think.

To do what, signior?

Signior Leonato, your niece regards me with an eye of favour. And I do with an eye of love requite her.

What's your will?

My will is this day to be conjoin'd in the state of honourable marriage; in which, good friar, I shall desire your help.

entreat your pains – ask a favour

My heart is with your liking.

And my help.

Here comes the Prince and Claudio.

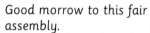

Good morrow to this fair assembly.

Are you yet determin'd today to marry with my brother's daughter?

I'll hold my mind.

Call her forth, brother; here's the friar ready.

Good morrow, Benedick. What's the matter, that you have such a February face, so full of frost, of storm, and cloudiness?

[*Enter Antonio, Hero, Beatrice, Margaret and Ursula. The women wear masks*]

Claudio: Which is the lady I must **seize upon**?

choose

Antonio: This same is she, and I do give you her.

Claudio: Why then she's mine. Sweet, let me see your face.

Leonato: No, that you shall not till you take her hand, before this friar, and swear to marry her.

Claudio: Give me your hand before this holy friar. I am your husband if you like of me.

Hero: [*Unmasking*] And when I liv'd, I was your other wife; and when you lov'd, you were my other husband.

Claudio: Another Hero!

Hero: One Hero died defil'd, but I do live, and surely as I live I am a maid.

Don Pedro: The former Hero! Hero that is dead!

Leonato: She died, my lord, but whiles her slander liv'd.

Friar: All this amazement can I **qualify**, when after that the holy rites are ended I'll tell you largely of fair Hero's death. To the chapel let us **presently**.

explain

(go) immediately

Benedick: Which is Beatrice?

Beatrice: [*Unmasking*] What is your will?

Benedick: Do you not love me?

Beatrice: No more than reason.

Benedick: Then your uncle, and the Prince, and Claudio have been deceiv'd – they swore you did.

Beatrice: Do you not love me?

Benedick: No more than reason.

Beatrice: Then my cousin, Margaret, and Ursula are much deceiv'd, for they did swear you did.

Benedick: They swore that you were almost sick for me.

Beatrice: They swore that you were well-nigh dead for me.

Benedick: Then you do not love me?

Beatrice: No, truly, but in friendly recompense.

Leonato: Come, cousin, I am sure you love the gentleman.

Claudio: And I'll be sworn that he loves her, for here's a paper written in his hand, a **halting sonnet** of his own pure brain, fashion'd to Beatrice.

bad poem

Hero: And here's another, writ in my cousin's hand, stol'n from her pocket, containing her affection to Benedick.

Benedick: A miracle! Here's our own hands against our hearts. Come, I will have thee, but by this light I take thee for pity.

Beatrice: I would not deny you, but by this good day I yield upon great persuasion, and partly to save your life, for I was told you were **in a consumption**.

ill

Benedick: Peace! I will stop your mouth.   [*He kisses her*] For thy part, Claudio, I did think to have beaten thee, but in that thou art like to be my kinsman, live unbruised, and love my cousin.

Claudio: I had well hoped thou wouldst have denied Beatrice, that I might have **cudgelled** thee out of thy single life.

beaten

Think about it

How might the audience be feeling now that a happy ending is in sight?

57